MW00943034

Contagious Courage

A 30-Day Journey to Overcoming Stress and Anxiety

Janet Perez Eckles

Contagious Courage: A 30-Day Journey to Overcoming Stress and Anxiety

Janet Perez Eckles
©Copyright 2014

All rights reserved solely by the author. The author guarantees all contents are original and do not infringe upon the legal rights of any other person or work. No part of this book may be reproduced in any form without the permission of the author.

Unless otherwise indicated, Scripture taken from the HOLY BIBLE, NEW INTERNATIONAL VERSION. Copyright © 1973, 1978, 1984, International Bible Society. Used by permission of Zondervan Bible Publishers.

Contagious Courage / Janet Perez Eckles. – 1st ed.

ISBN-13: 978-1505671537
ISBN-10: 1505671531

Table of Contents

Warning:

What you're about to read is a Christian book. Its pages might include graphic descriptions and explicit displays of God's power to transform, restore and heal.

Acknowledgments

Where would I be without my Lord, my King and Savior, best friend, Christ Jesus who understands, forgives, guides and overlooks my mistakes, flaws and foolish ways?

I relish in peace even in the midst of life's chaos because of His power at work in me.

I also acknowledge the man who cheers me on, who supports me, who never complains when asked to do the sometimes tedious tasks—Gene, my hubby of 39 years. He paints my heart with gratitude for his unconditional love.

To my Dad who sets an example of tenacity for me. And to my sweet, white-haired Mom whom we all call "Ita." Her unique charm is contagious when she scurries from here to there in the house and in the kitchen preparing meals for the family with the joy that sings from her heart.

And to my son, Jason, and his lovely wife Rachel who makes him happy. My two grandchildren who turned my life upside down with delight and my son Jeffrey--They all increase the richness of my days. My son Joseph, who lives in the glory of God's presence, adds to the expectation of heaven for me.

And I acknowledge that friends like Cindi Lynch, Jean Lane and Boots Rudd are the angels God sent fluttering to nudge me to my knees with deep gratitude.

Part I
Preparation

My dear friend, I just want to give you a great big ol' hug. Know why? Because that's what I needed when life turned ugly on me. I needed that friend to listen when my world became oh so dark. And stress and anxiety followed me everywhere. I longed for freedom from all that and also from the heartache that kept me awake at night.

You might be going through something similar. If you are, I hope to be that friend for you. That's why I wrote this book. We all know life is tough, impossible at times. And we need that someone who will sit beside us. Someone who will listen. And more importantly, we need a real-life example of a person who has walked along the same devastating path and has come out triumphant and shining with peace. And a person who, because of Christ, relishes with genuine joy.

Humbled with gratitude, I admit I fit that description. And thus, based on my first-hand experience with the darkest of valleys-- going blind at 31, enduring infidelity, the murder of my youngest son and the acquittal of the man responsible—all spelled misery for my life.

But God spelled the word "victory" instead.

What's in it for you?

Victory is the same word that could describe your life, and your situation. The fact you chose to open this book is a sign that you are ready to begin a new path, find another option, and learn a new way to bring back peace, shed that stress and anxiety. And with a smile in your heart, make your life shine.

But before it shimmers with victory, we recognize that we need one weapon. The weapon is courage.

Did you know that courage is the power that drips from God's Word for us to drink and face each unpredictable moment?

Ugly but true, Satan's job is to take away that courage or discourage, God's power infuses courage. And our job is to feel encouraged to keep going and never stop until we can say, "Through Christ I do have the strength to face anything" (Philippians 4:13).

How Did We Get Here?

Before we begin, we need to figure out how we got here in the first place. Some have spent countless nights, tossing in bed, tense, with the mind racing, hot with worry and fear. The next morning they wake up fatigued. Dragging their feet, they sit and drink a hot cup of stress and anxiety.

Goodness gracious, half the world ends up this way. But not you. Not anymore.

This book will take you day to day, for 30 days. And each day, you'll exercise the muscle of courage. The path is simple. Simple but not easy. It's not without effort, decision and commitment on your part.

Did you know that in life, we all belong to a certain kind of group? Here they are: those who wish for a better life. Those who know they want it. Those who watch others reach it. Those who live frustrated looking for it. But then there is the group of those who take action to make it happen.

And since you're reading these pages, you now belong to the "make-it-happen" group. I pushed my chair back and I'm on my feet, cheering for you, applauding your choice and rooting for your courageous resolve.

In this 30-day simple routine, you'll find courage is your friend. And you'll wake up to a new morning where that change will smile at you. You'll have the courage to leave that toxic relationship. Courage to declare freedom from that addiction. Courage to toss out that negative thinking, that harmful attitude, courage to say no more to paralyzing fear, searing guilt, oppression, or dominating circumstances. And with holy boldness, declaring you possess the courage to shout to the world that you're making a change and the new you is about to emerge.

What's Required?

So here we go. There are nearly 1,500 minutes in a day. And out of those minutes, only fifteen (15) minutes will be spent following this simple routine for 30 days. You'll begin a life of change. A life where a new door will open to set you free and walk down the solid path of courage. Up for the challenge? The answer will determine in which group you belong: survive with good intentions, or thrive with decisive action.

Someone read this on a tombstone: "Nelly had the notion to change right from the start. She never did. So here she sleeps with that desire in her heart."

For this change, each 15 minute session of the day will include these elements:

- *A theme

- A brief, real-life episode as an illustration

- A Bible verse

- A prayer

- Challenge questions

- A declaration

All you have to do is the following:

- Set your alarm clock 15 minutes before the normal time, or choose your lunchtime, or in the quiet of night.

- Find a place, private and silent

- Ask God to give you the wisdom to understand and the grace to begin the change

- Read the daily entry

- In your heart, or in a journal, jot your answers to the challenge questions. Why do this part? Because when you go back to read what you wrote, you will see just how much closer you are to the courageous new you.

Janet Perez Eckles

- With a voice of authority and out loud, repeat the "I declare" section. This is huge because when you speak words of power out loud, they become part of your thinking. They in turn, impact your attitude and subsequently, transform your demeanor, resulting in subtle yet delightful change in you.

- Last, tuck into your heart and into your mind what you learned in this exercise. And every moment your mind is free, ponder on the message you learned.

Note: Some folks start a plan like this, but give up. Know why? Because they miss a couple of days or a week and feel discouraged and never go back. It's okay to miss for reasons out of your control. The enemy, Satan, will cheer when you give up. But you will see the glory when you press on.

Part II
Taking Action

Day 1
The Correct Voice

I settled in my seat in the crowded church. The ventriloquist and his dummy's performance had everyone rolling with laughter.

How someone can be so talented and display that gift of humor is beyond me.

But in order to enjoy the show, this blind *chica* had to pay closer attention than the rest of the folks in the audience. Unable to see which one was talking, I needed to concentrate on the different sounds of the voices—of the dummy and the ventriloquist. Focusing on their sound allowed me to catch the humor.

You're probably doing the same. You're listening to voices, too. Not in a comedy show with a ventriloquist, but in daily life we're also in-tuned to three voices—your own self talk, God's Word and the enemy's voice.

This latter one often shouts louder —"See, you did it again, you'll never make it. Life is so hard, why even try? If you had a different past, today would be better. You don't have what it takes. No one has it harder than you. If you had your health, life would be better. You might as well give up."

That's the voice from the enemy. And if not alert, like dummies under his control, we might end up believing what we hear.

What if we concentrate on the voice that speaks truth, the voice that pronounces victory, the voice that claims the power that's in us? What if we made it a habit to listen to that voice that, as you read this, is whispering to you: "Do not fear, for I am with you; do not anxiously look about you, for I am your God. I will strengthen you, surely I will help you; surely I will uphold you with My righteous right hand" (Isaiah 41:10)?

Prayer

Father, how often I was tuned in to the wrong voice, receiving the wrong message and pondering on the destructive echo. My ears will be attentive to the power of your Word, to the pure message that promises no matter how bad things get, you'll hold me up, guide me, guard and keep me. In Jesus' name. Amen.

Reflection Questions

- What voice is speaking to you today?

- How will you choose to drown destructive voices?

Janet Perez Eckles

- Which of God's promises will echo in your mind today?

I Declare Out Loud

God is pleased with me. I declare to follow this 30-day simple plan. I choose to listen to His voice. No longer will the voice of discouragement or self-pity touch my ears. At every step I will trust in the power of God at work in me to silence anything that is not from Him. I have the courage to defeat any negative words and I will reject them and replace them with powerful, edifying, encouraging words that come from God.

Day 2
Crossing to the Land of Safety and Security.

With American passport in hand, my friend and I took in the action around the car. We inched our way in the long line of cars leaving Mexico, heading toward the U.S. border.

We experienced sensors which monitored each vehicle and signs to warn that all conversations inside the car were being recorded. Gulp.

My imagination ran wild. What if, like many stories we hear, they mistake us for, well...you know. What if!

After over an hour of stop and go traffic, an Immigration official approached the car. He asked for our passports and asked questions. We smiled shyly and answered all of them.

Minutes later, we reached the spot marked with yellow dots which defined the end of one country and the beginning of the other.

Once the car crossed that yellow-dotted line, we were officially in U.S. territory. My friend and I breathed a sigh of relief, a sigh of freedom.

You know that kind of freedom, don't you? Maybe you have crossed that line, too... when life seems to trap you with ugly junk,

Janet Perez Eckles

difficult people, uncertain promises, gloom on the horizon. And inching your way through life, you wonder when you'll reach the crossing line. When will you enter the land where things are peaceful? The territory that offers joy, genuine joy—not from the stuff we see, but from the wonder we hold inside. The place where, in spite of adversity, days shine with reassurance and hope.

Gotta tell you, I crossed that border when Jesus approached my vehicle and asked, "Where are you headed? And do you have the passport of faith?"

The answer was yes. A *resounding* yes. I had crossed the dotted line when I believed what the son of God said, what He offered and what He promised. As a citizen of this new land, I had the right to the same promise He made long ago: "If you hold to my teaching, you are really my disciples. Then you will know the truth, and the truth will set you free. So if the Son sets you free, you will be free indeed" (John 8:32, 36).

Prayer

Father, thank you for the new land you crafted for those who seek that freedom in you. I will make my home in the place where you rule, where you speak the truth, and where you govern under the constitution of your everlasting love. In Jesus' name. Amen.

Reflection Questions

- Where are you residing today?

- Is your passport of faith current?

- What keeps you from drawing closer to the border of the land He promised?

I Declare Out Loud

From this moment on, I will move forward to cross the line and step into the land of freedom. I shall embrace the freedom God prepared for me. I declare that I am indeed free from past wounds, dark memories, insults, abuse or mistakes. With the courage God gave me, I will reside in my new home where my courage shines and my days are bright.

Janet Perez Eckles

Day 3
Wishful Thinking

We took pictures, from every angle. Our granddaughter was the flower girl at my brother's wedding, so our camera was smoking from those umpteen pictures we took of our princess. We planned to send them to the world.

But all that planning fell apart. On the way home the camera slipped out of the console between the seats, right into a large cup of water.

We lifted the dripping camera. There went our pictures. There went our hopes of those priceless images.

To diffuse the tense moment, I gave a silly grin at hubby. "Maybe this is an underwater camera, and we just didn't know it?"

"Wishful thinking," he said.

That's me—the wishful thinker. I used to wish about lots of things. In fact, I wished my way would be the one that would bring me to heaven: By being good. By praying. By staying out of trouble. Through my religion. Or wishing God would be good enough to swing open heaven's doors and unable to resist my pitiful look, He'd say, "C'mon on, silly *chica*." I wished that.

Then some powerful truths evaporated my wishful, wrong thinking. God's truth—the spiritual GPS programmed my destination: Heaven.

The map showed two turns outlined in chapter 10 of Romans:

1. "If you confess with your mouth, 'Jesus is Lord' and if you

2. Believe in your heart that God raised him from the dead, you will be saved."

Prayer

Father, how awesome of you to make it so simple to be saved from hell and enter heaven. I confess there was a time when I doubted the path would be as simple. But now I know when I made the commitment to follow you, my heart was transformed. My life was changed. Joy was renewed. And hope for eternity turned to reality. I thank you in the name of Jesus. Amen.

Reflection Questions

- When you take your last breath, where will eternity find you?

- Are you like I was, wrong about the way to be saved from eternal gloom?

- Is Jesus knocking at the door of your heart?

I Declare Out Loud

Today I will change my wishful thinking for true, undeniable facts. I do possess the courage to lift my head and say "yes" to Jesus. With no reservations, I will turn away from the sin that tainted my life. And will make Jesus the Lord of all. I shall live secure of my eternity. And because I have that guarantee, today will begin a new life, triumphant and filled with courage to face anything.

Day 4
Trapped

Could I be as silly as these monkeys? I heard about folks in an exotic country who found a way to capture monkeys without harming them.

They place fruit inside a clear container. The monkeys smell the ripened fruit, stick in their thin arms and grab a fistful. Because the opening is narrow, they cannot pull their hairy hand back out.

That's when a net is draped over them. And *voila*! They're captured.

Have you been there? Me, too. When we hold tight to self-pity, the net of gloom is bound to cover us. When we hang on to discouragement, the net of despair is ready for us. When we grip resentment for old wounds, the net of bitterness is ready. And when we hold on to insecurities, the net of self-doubt is hovering over us.

We're trapped maybe because we're not any wiser than those monkeys. But good thing God knows our stubborn heart, our foolish ways and our human weakness to let go. We long for freedom, yet our grip is tight.

Janet Perez Eckles

But when the moment comes that we admit we're tired of the confinement, freedom through Jesus is found when we let go… "So if the Son sets you free, you will be free indeed" (John 1:8:36).

Prayer

Father, I confess being trapped by self-pity when I lost my sight. I hung on to bitterness and gloom. But your love set me free, free for me to fly with hope that turned to passion and joy. I thank you in the name of Jesus. Amen.

Reflection Questions

- Feeling trapped lately?

- What keeps you from recognizing what binds you?

- What will it take for you to let go and taste the freedom Jesus offers?

I Declare Out Loud

Today is when I will let go those bars that keep me trapped in self-pity. I am letting go of the toxic relationships, the harmful habits, the wrong attitude and any judgmental view. I now possess the courage to say "no" to flawed thinking and "yes" to God's liberating truth.

I am free. I am free indeed because Jesus set me free.

Day 5
Instant Gratification?

Recently, while slicing an apple, the kitchen knife slipped and I cut my finger. After the bleeding had stopped, my six-year-old granddaughter took a peek and gasped. But instantly, she placed her delicate hand to one side of the cut and held my hand with the other. "God, please heal my Nana's cut. Whenever you want, Lord. Maybe today, maybe tomorrow. Anytime you want, God."

Where did she learn that? Not from me. My prayers have a different tone: "Lord, can you perform that miracle yesterday?"

Although many decades ahead of my granddaughter, I'm learning from her. I shall learn to let God decide when the healing of searing heartache should begin. He'll know when the first moments of peace should come back, when the answers will be revealed, and when the desires of the heart will become reality.

And while taking each moment at a time, and even though I don't see the answer yet, this promise echoes that He sees, He observes and He hears my cries: "I waited patiently for the Lord; he turned to me and heard my cry." (Psalm 40:1)

Janet Perez Eckles

Prayer

Father, I confess impatience marked my attitude when I was desperate for an answer. Thank you for showing me the power of patience and the sweetness of waiting for your timing. In Jesus' name. Amen.

Reflection Questions

- What robs your peace while you wait?

- How can you increase your trust in God's perfect timing?

- What keeps you from trusting that He will give you the answer?

I Declare Out Loud

Today I will exchange my impatience for a peaceful waiting on the Lord. I will exercise courage to believe He is in control of all, of the outcome and all details. I have the certainty that God is at work in my situation. While I wait, I will receive His grace to make the waiting calm, joyous and filled with hope.

Day 6
Best Friend

Marty, my best friend during college was my maid of honor. What a sweet time it was back in those days. Through the years we honored our friendship and still share sweet moments together. Not as often, but we still trace memories of laughter. We recall silly moments when we disco danced, and shared joy during each other's weddings. We experienced sadness with sudden losses. And we understand each other's different views. We dabbed each other's tears at life's disappointments.

And sadly, sometimes those disappointments are part of friendship. They either build a strong bond or tear it apart. They bring us closer or put a wedge between us.

We cherish the friendship because we endured it all.

And although I didn't know Jesus during my college years, He became my friend years later. To my joy, His friendship has taken one more step to prove His love, His commitment and His promise:

"Greater love has no one than this that he lay down his life for his friends. You are my friends if you do what I command. I no longer call you servants, because a servant does not know his master's business. Instead, I have called you friends, for everything that I learned from my Father I have made known to you. You did not

Janet Perez Eckles

choose me, but I chose you and appointed you to go and bear fruit—fruit that will last" (John 15:16).

Prayer

Father, I confess I often disregard the greatest gift of your son, Jesus, who died for me, for my sins and for the eternal life that is now mine. When life fails me, when disappointments come and when darkness rules, I will remember what you did for me. I know you are the friend with the love that never ends, the support that never wanes and the power that never lessens. Thank you for being my greatest friend. In Jesus' name. Amen.

Reflection Questions

- Who is your best friend?

- What do you consider a good friend?

- What kind of friend are you?

I Declare Out Loud

Today I will begin by recognizing the Friend who gives me courage. When feeling alone, defeated or down, I will trust in Jesus, the friend who gave His life for me. I will count on His companionship to keep me encouraged, hopeful, secure and confident. When friends fail me, I will have the courage to trust in Him, and Him alone.

Day 7
First Thoughts

"Where is Papa?" my sleepy 5-year old granddaughter said the moment she opened her eyes in the morning.

"Papa already left for work," I said, grinning at her love for her Papa.

"I want to be with him…I just want a hug from him. I love him so much," she said.

After the sweetness of the moment faded, a not-too-sweet reminder came to mind. What about me? Do I ask for my Father's presence the first thing in the morning? Rather than my soul longing to be with God, in His presence and to seek His company, my thoughts often turn elsewhere.

How different it would be if I did wake up each morning with a yearning to be held by Him. To be reassured by Him. And to be guided by His grace.

God knows that weakness. He knows how we begin our day by dashing through daily tasks. And how we pour a cup of stress, add worry and stir in fear. He sees how we give in to restlessness at night.

But because He also knows how deeply we want peace, security and victory at every stage, He gives His direct instruction: "Seek

Janet Perez Eckles

first his kingdom and his righteousness, and all these things will be given to you" (Matthew 6:33).

Prayer

Father, I confess that worries fill my head when I wake up. I have been a fool to seek you only when troubles come, when challenges show up or gloom threatens to step in. I ask that you give me wisdom to first choose my thoughts and fill them with you every morning. In Jesus' name. Amen.

Reflection Questions

- What fills your mind when you open your eyes in the morning?

- What longing fills your heart?

- What is the order of your priorities lately?

I Declare Out Loud

Today I will receive the wisdom to begin my days with thoughts of the power that's at work in me. As a child of God, I have the courage to reject distractions that keep me from focusing on God, and to ponder His ways, His provision for my every need and His guidance toward victory. Today, my thoughts are directed to Him, to have success and prosperity shine in my life.

Day 8
Heed His Call

Time to change the bed sheets again. Our guest rooms get lots of use. And hubby and I have a passion and truly delight in hosting guests. Seldom does a month go by without us opening our home—a true joy!

Among our guests, we have had friends who are a bit shy. Some are fun. Some are uniquely interesting (such as the teenagers from Taiwan we hosted last year). And some, like my friend who is a hoot and, well, let's say…more than a tad bold.

She settled in our guest room on the second floor. On one occasion, in the still of the night, she heard a noise outside. Lifting the blinds, she peeked out the window and saw a group of teenagers. The scene seemed suspicious. They clearly were not from the area. All exited the car and began prowling. She opened the window a crack and gave an authoritative, loud shout: "Get back in that car!"

They froze. Then, frightened, they looked all around trying to determine the source of that order. In seconds, they dashed inside the car and took off.

I chuckled. And that night while trying to sleep, I wondered how many times God had also called out an order directed to me. But too busy in my prowling through life, I ignored it.

Janet Perez Eckles

Sometimes I get caught in the whirlwind of tasks and activities that, although He might be calling out guidance, options, directions, or warnings—it's hard to hear in the midst of busyness.

Yet, out of the window of heaven, He calls out: "I am he; I am he who will sustain you. I have made you and I will carry you; I will sustain you and I will rescue you." Isaiah 46:4

Prayer

Father, how often I missed when you called out reassurance and pronounced what I needed. Help me to be attentive to your call and open to hear the sweetness of your promises. In Jesus' name. Amen.

Reflection Questions

- How busy is your life today?

- What is God telling you lately?

- When is the last time you heard His voice speak to your soul?

I Declare Out Loud

Today is the day that I open my heart to hear His voice. I will have increased courage to say "no" to orders from the world and listen. Receive and fully embrace His sweet, yet powerful promises for me.

Day 9
Color it Victorious

Sometimes I'm just way too nosy. I met a new friend from Nigeria last week. And trying to get to know her, I bombarded her with questions about her culture.

"And what kind of food do you serve in your country?"

"Oh, vegetables, rice and all kinds of things...chicken mainly," she said. Then she chuckled. "We raise our own chickens. But we have to protect the chicks from birds that come and eat them."

"Really, how do you do that?"

"We paint them red," she said matter-of-factly. "That confuses the birds. They don't realize they're chicks."

Paint the chickens? How clever, I thought.

But on the serious side, sometimes we're like that—chicks, vulnerable, sort of innocent, clucking away, unaware of the enemy that is all too eager to have us for lunch. But covering us with a different color might just be the solution.

Here are three colors we might want to use:

Green. We have the go-ahead to trust in God's protection. Verses in Ephesians 6 give us the permission to wear the armor that guards against the enemy's attacks.

Red. To show the blood of Jesus that covers us from anguish that comes with difficult moments. We're protected from whatever tomorrow might bring. We're shielded from the uncertainty of the world's darkness.

Yellow. We're the light to the world. The struggles we endure are never to defeat us. But in turn, they will be the very reason for our light to shine with the triumph God will bring.

Walking with the color of victory painted on our soul, we live each moment with Jesus' reassurance that, "The thief comes only to steal and kill and destroy; I have come that they may have life, and have it to the full" (John 10:10).

Prayer

Father, I confess how often I went through my days, vulnerable, weak, lost and trembling. But now I know that you are present to guard and protect me. No more easy prey for the enemy. I walk secure, trusting, and relishing in the life, full and abundant that you promise. In Jesus' name. Amen.

Reflection Questions

- What is threatening your peace today?

- What will you do to protect yourself?

- How does your day change when you know you're shielded from the enemy's harm?

I Declare Out Loud

I declare that as a child of God, I am protected, I am guarded from evil, and I am shielded from what the world might have against me. With the power of God at work in me, I will not fear any words, attitudes, situations or conflicts to steal my joy or decrease my courage.

Janet Perez Eckles

Day 10
Use the Right Tool

If you lived in Bolivia in the 60's, a trip to the beauty shop for a haircut was an extreme luxury. So, what did my Mom do when I was little? She placed a bowl on my head and cut my bangs.

Gulp. I have proof of the outcome in pictures I found in the back of the closet, inside an album piled on top of others from decades ago.

Mom was doing her best. But she admitted she didn't use the right tool.

"It's okay, Mom," I said. "You used what you had."

But she's not alone. When it comes to measuring other things of life, we also use the wrong measuring tool.

For example, we grab the incorrect measuring stick when figuring out our level of happiness.

We gauge what a good life should be through the absence of problems. We calculate security by the size of our bank account. We measure joy with the lack of problems and struggles. And we compute the level of our peace with the absence of challenges.

May I be bit bold and ask you (and me too), to throw away that unreliable tool that is supposed to measure our degree of happiness?

The best way to measure is to gauge how close God is to our situation. How near He is to our heartache and how close He is to our anxiety. So using the yard stick of faith, we declare: "The Lord is near. Do not be anxious about anything, but in everything, by prayer and petition, with thanksgiving, present your requests to God. And the peace of God, which transcends all understanding, will guard your hearts and your minds in Christ Jesus" (Philippians 4:6).

Prayer

Father, how foolish I've been trying to measure how happy I was by using the world's guide. How feeble my thinking that life would be free of trials. But now I rejoice for I do have the tool, the perfect tool to destroy the stress and worry that get in the way of my joy, my peace and my security. In Jesus' name. Amen.

Reflection Questions

- What level of happiness marks your days?

- How do you measure them?

- What tool do you use to kill anxiety, fear and worry?

Janet Perez Eckles

I Declare Out Loud

I will erase any anxiety, stress or fear because God has control of my life, my days and my desires. Today, I will increase my courage to affirm that God is guarding my mind and heart. I have the courage to discard human tools to gauge happiness. Instead, at every chance, I will look to God's love for me that cannot be measured.

Day 11
Looking Up for the Scent of Peace

"I was walking in the garden, between rows of purple flowers," my friend said. "Then I caught the scent of a delightful fragrance." She followed the scent, trying to figure out where it came from. She looked all around to the right, to the left, through various rows of flowers, around corners, in the back, toward the front.

Then, she happened to look up. There it was! Almost as high as the electric wires, lilac bushes formed a canopy above her, giving off that exquisite scent.

Have you done that too? Looking for the place where you can find the scent of prosperity, of happiness, of joy, of peace. Sometimes, a lifetime is spent looking, and looking.

And when we happen to lift our eyes and look up—to the giver of all that's beautiful and colorful, bathed in the fragrance of pure love, we find the source. "Your love, O LORD, reaches to the heavens, your faithfulness to the skies. Your righteousness is like the mighty mountains, your justice like the great deep." Psalm 36:5-6a

Prayer

Father, I confess how much time I wasted, looking in the wrong places for what I needed. But when I look up, I find what fills me,

Janet Perez Eckles

what satisfies and what brings the delightful scent of contentment. In Jesus' name. Amen.

Reflection Questions

- Where have you been looking for fulfillment?

- What have you found in your search?

- What happens when you pause and look beyond the world's call?

I Declare Out Loud

Today, I will stop searching; looking for deceptive answers and lures. My eyes will first be upon God's mighty ways. I will receive the courage I need, the peace I long for, and the contentment for which my heart hungers.

Day 12
Recalculate

Technology is getting uncomfortably invasive. The ability for a GPS system to identify your exact location is a bit creepy.

And what if I were to tweet from a hotel room, would the world know where I am?

Am I being a tad paranoid about my privacy? Maybe so. But what about God's GPS? He has been tracking all details from the beginning. He follows each move you and I make. And He tracks the insecurities, the hidden frustrations, and even the worry we hide behind a smile.

Our tough moments are familiar to Him, and so are the secrets we tucked way inside. He's aware of all–the good and the bad. But "The days of the blameless are known to the LORD, and their inheritance will endure forever. In times of disaster they will not wither; in days of famine they will enjoy plenty" (Psalm 37:1).

Prayer

Father, days of disaster are all around. Adversity is at every corner. But I thank you for the power of your forgiveness when we repent. And I thank you that you gave us the way to live a blameless life so we would enjoy plenty even in times of famine. In Jesus' name. Amen.

Reflection Questions

- What secrets do you hide in your heart?

- How will you release them to the Lord?

- How reassured do you feel knowing He's watching your every move?

I Declare Out Loud

Today is when I will stand clean and free because all my intimate secrets, darkest sin and many mistakes are known to the Lord. He accepts my repentance, He forgives, He forgets my sin and He prepares the best for me. With that reassurance, I stand with courage to face whatever tomorrow will bring.

Day 13
Eternal Longevity

Chew coca leaves every day? Who would do a crazy thing like that? Well, a 123-year-old man still alive gives his reasons:

Reuters: "Bolivia — Bolivian indigenous farmer Carmelo Flores, who could be the oldest person to have ever lived, attributes his longevity to quinoa grains, riverside mushrooms and around-the-clock chewing of coca leaves."

Being from Bolivia, I grew up eating quinoa. And chewing coca leaves by the indigenous population is as common as riots in the streets of La Paz.

But whether we live in downtown streets of New York or in the rural areas of Bolivia, the number of years we live on this earth makes no difference, has no meaning or significance.

The only thing that matters is that each day we know in Whose hands we are, in Whose will we operate, and Whose plan we follow.

Rather than the number of birthdays, each moment counts. Each day can impact someone. And each season of our lives delivers a message to those around us.

What message and legacy is your life tracing? Why does each minute count? Because "As for man, his days are like grass, he

Janet Perez Eckles

flourishes like a flower of the field; the wind blows over it and it is gone, and its place remembers it no more. But from everlasting to everlasting the LORD's love is with those who fear him, and his righteousness with their children's children – with those who keep his covenant…" (Psalm 103:15-18).

Prayer

Father, with each birthday I celebrate, I want to rejoice because each year brings me closer to the destination you planned. I want to focus not on the length of my days, but on the strength you give me and the power that's at work within me to face each moment. In Jesus' name. Amen.

Reflection Questions

- How long would you like to live?

- What is your life revealing so far?

- Are you counting on God's power at work within you to face each moment?

I Declare Out Loud

Today will begin the legacy I will leave behind. Those in my life will know that in the midst of hardship, I had the courage to keep going, to trust in God, to believe and live with peace in my soul.

Day 14
Teaching Tools

I drew my five-year-old granddaughter closer to me. We held hands. "C'mon, honey, we need to pray." That's how we begin each day... asking God to rebuke any spirit of disobedience or laziness. She learned the word "rebuke" early on.

The task of helping to home school her is at times tough and challenging. But mostly it's delightfully rewarding. At times I need to be sweet. Others, firm. And even at times, forceful as a tigress.

Admittedly, God deals with me in the same pattern. He varies His approach. When my flawed whims take me in the wrong direction, He whispers the correction. When fear knocks at the door, He repeats His promises. But when crisis shakes my world, the power of His commanding voice can't be ignored.

Maybe He's doing that right now in your life, in your circumstance, and in your longing. He's not just sweetly whispering but firmly asserting this command: "Have I not commanded you? Be strong and courageous. Do not be terrified; do not be discouraged, for the LORD your God will be with you wherever you go" (Joshua 1:9).

Janet Perez Eckles

Prayer

Father, so often I do need your stern commands, and your firm instructions. When filled with fear and anxiety. When the road is rough, I will receive your order to be reassured, to be confident that you are with me. In Jesus' name. Amen.

Reflection Questions

- How do you react to God's commands?

- What is He saying to you right now?

- What reassurance do you find when you know God will be with you at every stage?

I Declare Out Loud

Today I will obey His command to be courageous, to be bold and to walk with certainty in the territory of adversity. I declare that fear will not stop me or terrify me. Instead, I take firm steps on the path He traced for me.

Day 15
Shark Attack

3D movies are pretty cool, unless you're blind. But just because I can't see doesn't mean I would miss the opportunity for my five-year-old granddaughter to enjoy the delightful show at SeaWorld.

No sir, holding on to her hand, we made our way into the theatre. The music blasted, the sounds bounced through the walls. And at first, she was mesmerized, twirling all around to catch the images in the 360-degree screen.

But then the music reached a crescendo. She clung to me, digging her little face in my chest. "I'm scared, Nana. The sharks are getting me."

I wrapped my arms around her. "It's okay. They look close to you because of the glasses you're wearing."

We're also fooled when facing the sharks of problems, aren't we? Adversity seems to be so close that you cringe and tremble. And thinking it will bite your security away, God's voice echoes: "It's the 3D glasses you're wearing—they're human, flawed and limited. The view is different with me. My scenery is divine. The reality of my plan for your life has another image—not yours, but my own, unique for you."

Janet Perez Eckles

His reminder of His protection repeats over and over again. His shield from the danger is firm. And His guard from harm is as certain as His word: "Therefore do not worry about tomorrow, for tomorrow will worry about itself. Each day has enough trouble of its own" (Matthew 6:37).

And when today's troubles come, we trust in Him for the solution. And with new clarity, we watch through the glasses of faith to see how threats vanish.

Prayer

Father, how often I've trembled at the thought of tomorrow's potential problems. But now I thank you that because of your promises, I can take off those glasses that distort the view. I rejoice knowing that the screen plays your scenes. It shows you holding me in your hands, placing your arms of security and confidence around my worried heart. Thank you for the happy ending you always bring when I trust in you. In Jesus' name. Amen.

Reflection Questions

- What kind of glasses are you wearing these days?

- Where will you look for refuge?

- Who holds the security for your life?

I Declare Out Loud

Today, I will see my circumstance through the eyes of God—they will seem small compared to His power. I will not wear the glasses of worry, but rather the glasses that magnify His hand at work in every detail of my circumstance.

Janet Perez Eckles

Day 16
A Personal Note

That's what friends are for... to share the painful, the silly, the joyous and the sad. Years ago my dear friend related the problems with her husband. He had been harsh, cold and less-than-sensitive with her. But once in a while, he sent her warm notes and flowers. Yet his behavior didn't change. The notes were loving, but cold was his treatment towards her.

Her wise response to his unchanging pattern stuck in my head: "I need you to be the note," she said to him.

That request stirred in my memory a powerful truth—God's Word is Himself revealed. Each verse is Him loving us. Each message is Him whispering comfort to our heartache. His every admonishing is building our protection. And with every promise, He snuggles against our soul to brush sweet peace for our nights.

His Word is the loveliest note written with His love. What a fool I had been to go through my day and head to bed without savoring those personal notes.

But when taking the time to delight in them, we receive them. We read them. We believe in them and count on them; then the Word becomes His voice and He becomes the person who ushers triumph over every struggle.

And claiming that victory, my response, my note to Him is: "My heart is steadfast, O God; I will sing and make music with all my soul" (Psalm 105:1).

Prayer

Father, I thank you that no matter how the world treats me, how harsh the situations and vicious evil attacks can be, I can make music because of you. I can sing joy because of your Word, and I can fill my nights with peace because of your comfort. In Jesus' name. Amen.

Reflection Questions

- What makes your heart sing?

- What portion of God's promise brings peace to your soul?

- What note would you write back to God?

I Declare Out Loud

I will take time to read God's personal notes written to me. I will believe what He says. I will have the courage to embrace each message. I declare they will enrich my soul. I believe my life will reflect a renewed luster because I carry God's divine notes in my heart.

Janet Perez Eckles

Day 17
Where Credit is Due

Recently, admiration sang in my heart. Salon No. 8 at an Orlando hotel was jammed. Standing room only. And the buzz in the room quieted when he made his way to the front.

I sat on the front row beside my good friend. The session began as Senator Marco Rubio, with eloquence few possess, detailed the issues in his heart, his concern and in his commitment.

The issues he discussed stirred my heart.

But what nearly jolted me from my seat was this statement: When asked about running in the next presidential election, he said he'd pray on that decision and ask his family. He would do that because by then his children would be older and able to contribute to the decision. He added, "It's in God's hands. He hasn't always given me what I wanted. But He always gave me what I needed."

"Hats off to you for that conviction, Senator Rubio," I wanted to say. I admire those who have courage enough to give God the credit, tossing aside the fear of being politically incorrect.

Whether running for President of the United States, or running for the next promotion at work, or running from the troubles of life, this Word still resonates with powerful truth: "He alone is my rock and my salvation; he is my fortress, I will never be shaken" (Psalm 62:2).

Prayer

Father, in the race to reach the next level in my journey may I never trust in my abilities, skills or talents alone. But in you alone may I find strength, wisdom and security. In Jesus' name. Amen.

Reflection Questions

- What is the source for your convictions?

- Where do you draw wisdom from?

- How does the world's message influence your confidence?

I Declare Out Loud

From now on, I know God will provide for all I need. I know the decisions to be made will be guided by His Word. I will be confident that He gives me the wisdom to make decisions that honor Him. I will not doubt that His provision is with me every moment.

Day 18
Storm Shelter

Hubby grabbed my hand to begin our daily walk in our neighborhood park. "What do you think?" I said holding my other hand out to feel the light drips of rain.

"It's only a light drizzle," he said. "Let's go."

So off we went, diligent to walk off those extra calories. But while making our second round on the walking path, with no warning, the light drizzle turned to a downpour. We dashed to the nearest picnic area and plopped on a bench under the roof.

But we got wet anyway. The strong wind blew the rain from the sides.

Oh my, my, that wasn't the first time that happened to me. I had done the very same thing before. When trouble and heartache poured into my life, I ran for cover under God's protection. And I sought shelter under His comfort.

But the wind of human doubt and worry blew gloom into my aching heart.

Have you been there? Facing turmoil, you turn to God. And you know you're sure He protects you. You're certain about The One who is your shelter...but still that wind of doubt and human insecurity brings in the rain of fear.

Contagious Courage   55

But in that fear, we have company. David did the same: "My heart is in anguish within me; the terrors of death assail me. I said, 'Oh, that I had the wings of a dove! I would fly away and be at rest. I would hurry to my place of shelter, far from the tempest and storm'" (Psalm 55:4, 6, 8).

But his anguish changed as ours should too while we sing in the sunshine of God's security: "God is our refuge and strength, an ever-present help in trouble. Therefore we will not fear, though the earth gives way and the mountains fall into the heart of the sea, though its waters roar and foam and the mountains quake with their surging" (Psalm 46:1-3).

Prayer

Father, I confess that I foolishly allowed the winds of doubt to come into my peaceful shelter. I will rest in your promise that you are my ever-present help in trouble, in turmoil and in trying times. I will count on your powerful protection. In Jesus' name. Amen.

Reflection Questions

- What do you need protection from these days?

- Who offers you the comfort in the storms of life?

- How will you deepen your trust in God's protection for tomorrow?

Janet Perez Eckles

I Declare Out Loud

Today I will stand strong against any doubt. I will feel secure under the umbrella of His love. I will not succumb to the winds of adversity. God is my shelter and I am protected from the storms that may come my way.

Day 19
Ability

"I don't know how you do it," I said to my sister-in-law. She handles her deafness as the triumphant lady that she is.

She chuckled. "What do you mean?" Then she added, "I don't know how you do it. Being blind must be so hard. But you manage to do so much."

Although her words of encouragement regarding my blindness touched me, I'm in awe at the way she triumphed beyond her deafness to reach professional and personal success.

That night, I thought about us being together—the deaf and the blind. But we laugh, we joke, we love each other and have delightful moments shopping, eating dinner out and relaxing by the pool.

And the secret for our joy is in the exchange we both choose to make. Should our disabilities get in the way, rather than allow discouragement to slither in, we choose to come to Jesus. To seek Him. To count on Him. And to rely on His power and might. And time and time again, we accept Jesus' invitation:

"Come to me, all you who are weary and burdened, and I will give you rest. Take my yoke upon you and learn from me, for I am

Janet Perez Eckles

gentle and humble in heart, and you will find rest for your souls. For my yoke is easy and my burden is light" (Matt. 11:28-30).

Prayer

Father, no matter what disabilities, what challenges and what hurdles we have in life, it's peace that we seek. And in moments of difficulties, we will find rest for our souls in You and in the gentleness of Your Word. In Jesus' name. Amen.

Reflection Questions

- What obstacles are you facing now?

- How long will you carry your burden?

- Have you felt peace in your soul lately?

I Declare Out Loud

Today, I will face my weakness as God's channel to make me strong. I will embrace any disability—physical or emotional—to be used by God in a mighty way. I will have the courage to keep moving forward with resolve, with passion and contentment.

Day 20
One Nation Under God

Red, white and blue, barbecue, potato salad, and apple pie—that's on my menu for the 4th of July. And in my heart I have fireworks of gratitude bursting because a few decades ago my parents chose to make the U.S. our home.

That's why my friend's comment jolted me. "I would never become a U.S. citizen," she said.

Really? When my family landed in this country, our dream was to become American citizens.

Although that decision had a price—we had to renounce our Bolivian citizenship—the choice was as easy as the U.S. was our home.

Things have changed. People can now have dual citizenship. But that makes no sense to me. Pledging allegiance to two countries dilutes the commitment.

You don't agree with me? That's okay. Promising to be committed to one entity, one nation, one government and one faith makes our devotion strong and firm.

But who am I kidding? I had done the very same thing—pledged my allegiance to Christ, to be His follower. But still looked back at my mistakes, claiming I'm a Christian, yet falling for the temptations

60   Janet Perez Eckles

just like before. Believing in God's truth for reassurance, yet still looking back at yesterday's failures. Understanding His forgiveness, yet cringing at my sin.

How about you? When Jesus whispered to your soul, "Follow me"...did you nod your head and commit to do so completely and fully? Or were you like this man:

He (Jesus) said to another man, "Follow me." But he replied, "Lord, first let me go and bury my father."

Jesus said to him, "Let the dead bury their own dead, but you go and proclaim the kingdom of God." Still another said, "I will follow you, Lord; but first let me go back and say goodbye to my family."

Jesus replied, "No one who puts his hand to the plow and looks back is fit for service in the kingdom of God" (Luke 9:59-62).

Prayer

Father, I look to my feeble commitment and ask for wisdom to make my allegiance to you complete and constant. I thank you that you still love me even when I'm tempted to look back. In Jesus' name. Amen.

Reflection Questions

- What are you still holding on to?

- Have you tasted the freedom when Jesus becomes your Lord?

- What keeps you from fully committing to Him?

I Declare Out Loud

Today I will affirm my courage to leave the past behind and live as the citizen of God's Kingdom. I will have the conviction not to fall back into old habits, old toxic relationships, old damaging thoughts. I pledge my allegiance to God's ways, clean, pure and worthy.

Day 21
Purification

I stood at the kitchen table. "You gotta be kidding!" I said to hubby.

Why is it that bills never stop? We just got a notice that our water filter under the kitchen sink needs to be changed. As much as I hate to pay this extra charge, the decision to take this step was clear when the installer pulled out the old, dingy filter. It had trapped all the impurities, toxins and harmful chemicals of the water.

My life mirrored that same gadget. I resisted changing it, too. The effort to live a clean life takes time and the task requires work.

On the outside, I go through life pretending all is clear and free of contaminants. But reality is that junk has accumulated; stuff has been trapped for a long time, maybe for years.

Most won't see it...but I know they're there—insecurities, selfishness, doubt, anxiety, envy, impatience—the filter is looking pretty dingy.

But sooner or later God sends a notice—the need to change is now. The time to clean is clear. And the way to purify from the junk is available.

But although the change is possible, it's impossible on our own. So He sent the divine installer. To set us free. To give a clean start. To bring the freshness of a new life: "[Jesus Christ] gave himself for us to redeem us from all wickedness and to purify for himself a people that are his very own, eager to do what is good" (Titus 2:14).

Prayer

Father, for years I lived a life clogged with so much that my days were heavy with accumulated junk. I thank you for the perfect cleansing you provide, the permanent way to rid of sin. And the ever-present reminder that I need you to keep my heart clean. In Jesus' name. Amen.

Reflection Questions

- What needs cleaning in your life?

- Whose help will you count on?

- How deep is your desire to live a worry-free, fear-free life?

I Declare Out Loud

Today is the beginning of cleaning. I remove anything that had clogged my heart from feeling clean. I draw from God the courage to identify what has stained my soul. And I resolve to keep my heart clean, free from the debris of sin.

Janet Perez Eckles

Day 22
Faith Filling Station

This past Sunday, hubby and I headed to the beach to visit friends and catch some sun rays. But the excitement of the trip turned cold when the computer display on the dash showed we had only 14 miles to go before the tank was empty. Gulp. Nothing but highway ahead.

The 14 soon turned to 10. We prayed. Then the indicator turned to 5. Then 2. No gas stations, or exits anywhere either.

Finally, the displayed showed zero miles. That's when I swallowed what I might have said and instead spoke softly. "Honey, God still works miracles." I fidgeted in my seat. "A gas station will appear somewhere soon."

"We're going on fumes," he said. He was sweating and so was I. We had turned the air off to conserve gas.

I thought it to be an impossible situation. I don't know how but the car still moved down the highway on zero gas. We passed one mile marker, then another. No civilization anywhere.

Until a sign appeared at a distance. Sure enough, we took the next exit and there it was—a Mobil station.

Do I believe in miracles? Yes. But before you think I'm a strong, faith-filled Christian, think again. I had already pulled out my cell to

Contagious Courage

call AAA. You see...I said I believed in miracles, but inside, I was going to take action to remedy the situation on my own.

You might have done that too—faced an impossible situation, out of your control. The heat of pain scorches. And nowhere do you see signs of healing or solutions. So you say that you believe. You want to trust. You display convictions. Express assurance. But deep down, your faith has fumes of doubt.

It's okay. God knows. That's why He said, "I tell you the truth, if you have faith as small as a mustard seed, you can say to this mountain, 'Move from here to there and it will move. Nothing will be impossible for you'" (Matthew 17:21).

Prayer

Father, impossible situations abound, mountains of heartache stand in the way, and difficulties line the highway of life. But in you will I put my faith, though small, but it will sustain me until I find the station that fills my soul with reassurance and gratitude. In Jesus' name. Amen.

Reflection Questions

- What seems impossible to you today?

- What assurance do you have that God is watching over the details and is in control?

- How do you remove doubt from your heart?

Janet Perez Eckles

I Declare Out Loud

Today, I will stop trying to use my own abilities, my ways and my skills to resolve impossible situations. Instead, I will have the courage to believe, to truly believe in miracles. I will call upon God's power to intervene and I will wait in expectation for the outcome.

Day 23
Flats on the Road to Glory

What happens when you have a 3-year-old, a thumbtack and a rubber Pilate's ball? You guessed it—trouble. Before I could stop him, his little hand went to action. And my sturdy, wonderful ball on which I sit while working on my computer went flat in just minutes. I lifted the limp piece of rubber and tossed it in the trash.

But that wasn't the first time. Life did that to me too—when I lost my sight, when my son was killed. Heartache took my breath away, leaving me flat with deep suffering and sorrow.

But rather than tossing me in the trash of misery, God lifted me, gave me the breath of hope. He filled me with His comfort. He showed me how to deal with suffering; and He put back all I needed inside to bounce back with peace, with confidence and joy.

He does that, you know, for anyone who trusts that He will, who believes that He can, and receives what He offers.

In the midst of your suffering, in the middle of your pain, and the darkness of your valley, you're not left flattened with hopelessness because He promised "the God of all grace, who called you to his eternal glory in Christ, after you have suffered a little while, will himself restore you and make you strong, firm and steadfast" (1 Peter 5:10).

Janet Perez Eckles

Prayer

Father, how often I was stuck with a stubborn pride that brought misery my way. I failed to believe how you heal our suffering. But I believe in your Word and will trust in you to turn my weakness to strength, to make me firm and sturdy to face whatever comes my way. In Jesus' name. Amen.

Reflection Questions

- What has punctured and flattened your joy?

- What have you found to be the answer?

- In whom will you trust to restore you?

I Declare Out Loud

Today, I declare that I will face my suffering with the courage that opens my heart to hear from God. When tempted to sink in self-pity, I will be strong and affirm that God is at work. God is rebuilding. God is healing. And I declare that the new me is emerging.

Day 24
Blind Faith

I hate, hate it when the church service is about to begin, and I need to visit the ladies room. Hubby leads his blind wife to the entrance and waits for me. I usually make my way out with no problem. Sometimes I take a while because I chat with friends—girl stuff, you know.

And when I walk out, all I have to do is stretch my hand before me. And without fail, in seconds, hubby's strong hand grips mine and off we go.

Since I lost my sight that has been our routine. I never doubt he'll be there. I never hesitate to reach out to him. I don't see him with my physical eyes, but have faith he'll be there.

But shame, shame on me. I confess that faith in my husband doesn't transfer to the same faith in God's presence.

Have you done that? Put immense faith in an earthly thing or person? But when it comes to blindly trusting God...a different story, right? Why do we doubt He'll be ready to take our hand? Why do we have reservations about trusting He's indeed beside us? Why do we fret, thinking we're alone with our worries? Why do we hesitate to reach out?

Janet Perez Eckles

Life would be sweeter and look better if we changed our approach: "I will praise the LORD, who counsels me; even at night my heart instructs me. I have set the LORD always before me. Because he is at my right hand, I will not be shaken" (Psalm 16:7-8).

Prayer

Father, I'm trying to increase my trust in you. When life gets complicated, I can't seem to find my way out and the path looks dark, I shall trust in you. I will increase my faith to know your hand is outstretched to guide me and lead me to quiet places. I will believe that you are near me. I shall not be shaken. In Jesus' name. Amen.

Reflection Questions

- In whom do you put your trust when life gets tough?

- Who leads you out of troubled times?

- How do you find God's presence?

I Declare Out Loud

Today will be the beginning of a new, deep trust in God's hand. I will have courage because I'm not alone. No matter what I face, what unknown comes tomorrow, or what temptation lures, I will stand firm and not be shaken.

Day 25
Activation

More than a tad embarrassed, I took the credit card back. "It's been declined," the restaurant clerk had said.

I forced a smile and rumbled in my purse. "Let me see if I have another one."

Why would that card be declined? I had just received it as a gift a week prior.

When I inquire about it, the answer made me blush even more. "You have to call the number on the back of the card and activate it before trying to use it."

Sigh! What a silly detail. But one that made all the difference.

Sort of like the way we try to tap into God's Word. We read it, keep it and try to use it. But it doesn't bring results.

And it's because we often miss that detail. The step or the secret that makes all the difference – It won't work until we *believe* His Word.

When we do believe it, that's when it becomes active in our lives. We can then count on its power. That's when we can obtain freedom. Acquire peace. And attain victory.

Janet Perez Eckles

That's why, when facing difficulties, here is the question to ask: "Who is it that overcomes the world? Only he who believes that Jesus is the Son of God" (1 John 5:5).

Prayer

Father, how often I want to overcome my troubles, to triumph, to succeed but fail to truly believe that you are the one who can achieve all this through me. I thank you for the richness of your promise that we can overcome when we activate our faith in you. In Jesus' name. Amen.

Reflection Questions

- How will you activate genuine faith?

- What doubt still lingers in you?

- How will you overcome the challenges in life?

I Declare Out Loud

Today I affirm that I have the faith to believe, the courage to receive and the resolve to activate and apply God's Word in all circumstances I face today. I refuse to doubt. I declare my new genuine belief in the power of God at work in me.

Day 26
Your Book

Recently, my dear friend and I stepped into a nice hotel nestled in the busy part of Miami, near the airport. She put a large gift basket in my hands. "I think they left this for you."

What a lovely surprise! And on the night table was a stand with a copy of my new release, <u>Simplemente</u> <u>Salsa</u>, to be launched at EXPOLIT (an annual event for publishers, bookstores, music artists and distributors—an event too huge for my brain to take in).

I removed the cellophane, lifted items out of the basket and grinned with delight. Then a thought slipped in my head: that's what heaven will be like—we step into the room Jesus prepared. A delicious and delightful gift waits for us. And beside it, there it sits—the book we wrote with our lives.

A lovely thought...until we examine what would fill the pages of that book. Gulp.

Would it highlight the accomplishments of our life? Would it show the details of what we bought? Would it relate the stuff we accumulated? Or will it illustrate that we simply loved God with all our heart, mind and soul?

The time to step into that house in heaven isn't far. So we assess the writing. We edit our days and correct any mistaken worry. And with resolve, we erase any unfounded fear. And blot out ways that lead us from God's path. And definitely, take out any hints of worldly whims and empty desires.

So, being a little bold, may I ask: What will your book contain? Will you page through and smile with its contents as it's displayed on the night table in the house Jesus prepared for you? In case the changes are extensive, Jesus says: "Do not let your hearts be troubled. Trust in God; trust also in me. In my Father's house are many rooms; if it were not so, I would have told you. I am going there to prepare a place for you" (John 14:1-2).

Prayer

Father, let me fill the pages of my life's book with entries that make you smile, bring delight to you and form a sweet fragrance unto you. In Jesus' name. Amen.

Reflection Questions

- What are you writing with your life?

- Do you ever ponder the purpose of your days?

- Is there anything you need to have Jesus delete from the pages of your book?

I Declare Out Loud

Today is the day I affirm the guarantee of heaven for me. The book I write with my life highlights the courage that now fills my heart, which directs my steps and accomplishes all God had planned for me.

Janet Perez Eckles

Day 27
I was Blind and Now I See

"You're a fake," a new friend said to me. She did...to my face.

What else could I do, but laugh?

Actually we both laughed because of what she added, "I don't think you're really blind. You handle yourself so well. Put on your own make-up, fix your hair...I can't believe you're blind."

What a sweet compliment. She became my new best friend.

But what she doesn't know is that there was a time when I was a real fake, sighted and fully confident—on the outside. But a confused *chica* rumbled inside.

I was confused because I thought attending church every Sunday would make me good. My college degrees would bring security. Popularity would bring joy. And a good figure and a decent wardrobe would bring confidence.

Not so. I looked around for that truth, one which would fill my soul and ease my longings. Then, it happened. My eyesight closed up and my spiritual eyes opened. I read the truth. The truth that gave me rich life—and kept me dancing with meaning:

"I am the way and the truth and the life. No one comes to the Father except through me" (John 14:6).

Prayer

Father, there are so many options to follow and so many voices that whisper the way to truth. Thank you for the eyes you gave me to see the *only* way, the only truth and the only life is found in your Son Jesus. In His name I thank you.

Reflection Questions

- How long have you been looking for truth?

- What is the truth that fills your heart?

- Does your life reflect the truth you embrace?

I Declare Out Loud

Today, I discard any false or fake ways about me. I declare freedom. I will shine with the real me, the courageous me, and the faith-filled me. The world will see God's shining truth in all I do.

Janet Perez Eckles

Day 28
I Sought the Lord and the Lord Won

Was it beautiful? Gorgeous? Or simply stately? All of the above describe my friend's home at an exquisite location on one of the scenic Florida canals.

But what also impressed me was the sound system. The oldies played and the catchy melody followed me to the pool area, inside, in the kitchen, and in the bedrooms. No matter where, the sweet tunes played.

Then I stopped. Goodness gracious. I had the same sound system deep in my heart. Here is what it played:

1. A bit ashamed to admit but decades ago, when I disregarded Jesus' power and swam in the pool of my own abilities and accomplishments, He reminded me: "Pride goes before destruction, a haughty spirit before a fall. The LORD detests all the proud of heart. Be sure of this: They will not go unpunished" (Proverbs 18:5).

2. When I walked into the bedroom of fear, insecurity and uncertainty, God's Word played: "I sought the LORD, and he answered me; he delivered me from all my fears" (Psalm 34:4).

3. I stepped into the kitchen where all my passion and love poured into preparing the best life for me. But His word said: "'Teacher, which is the greatest commandment in the Law?' Jesus replied: 'Love the Lord your God with all your heart and with all your soul and with all your mind'" (Matthew 22:36-37).

Prayer

Father, thank you for evicting me from the house of destructive pride and inviting me to dwell in your house of security. My fears are washed away. And my insecurities cleaned. I relish in my dwelling where the home is covered by the insurance of life eternal with you. In Jesus' name. Amen.

Reflection Questions

- What melody plays in the rooms of your heart?

- In moments of fear who comes to your rescue?

- In whom do you place your trust for a secure life?

I Declare Out Loud

I refuse to be guided by pride any longer. I declare that my humility before God will turn to the strength He gives me, to the heights He will take me, and to the joy He will pour upon me.

Janet Perez Eckles

Day 29
Housekeeping

"Quick, Honey," I said, "get your shoes in the closet, and make sure the remote controls aren't all over the place."

The videographer from a local TV network affiliate was about to arrive. And the clips were to be used as part of my intro as I keynoted an event.

So I dashed to and fro making sure the house was pretty tidy.

Crazy isn't it? Why don't I worry about cleaning my heart, my attitude, my habits and my complaining tendencies with that same urgency?

That should be my priority as God doesn't need a video camera. He's already there, sitting on the sofa of my heart. He's observing where I put my faith, where I tuck my trust and how much joy I store in this life of mine.

I made a decision—to make sure my heart is tidy "For the eyes of the Lord range throughout the earth to strengthen those whose hearts are fully committed to him" (II Chronicles 16:9).

Prayer

Father, even though my life isn't perfect, my flaws are evident, my weaknesses real. Help me to have a heart that is perfectly clean for you. In Jesus' name. Amen.

Reflection Questions

- What needs cleaning up in your life?

- What will you do to make the needed changes?

- What will fill your heart today?

I Declare Out Loud

Today I will ponder to identify what areas in my life need re-arranging, the priorities that need to be re-ordered, and the goals and dreams that need to align with God's plans. I do have the courage to wait upon the Lord to make His plans known to me.

Janet Perez Eckles

Day 30
Cleanse with Living Water

My friend confessed to me. "Here is why I know I am falling short on wise counsel—because I tend to blame everyone else but me. When I can't find my car in the parking lot, my first thought is NOT to think that I could have misplaced it...it is to wonder who would have the nerve to steal a 15-year-old car. Naturally, the result is that I forgot where I put it."

My problem is contrary to my friend's. I tend to blame myself for all that might go wrong. Correction: I used to be that way. The "I'm so dumb," or "I did it again" or "how could I have done or said that" rumbled in that worried head of mine.

The blame, the negative self-talk left me drained, exhausted really. The outcome was a dried up, withered *chica*, thirsty for acceptance and approval. And to make things worse, even at night, I placed my head on the pillow of guilt.

What relief filled me when I learned that Jesus knew. And He offered the way to rinse out self-damaging notions. To wash out tainted self-talk. And instead, refresh my soul with living water.

"Let anyone who is thirsty come to me and drink. Whoever believes in me, as the Scripture has said, rivers of living water will flow from within him" (John 7:37-38).

Prayer

Father, I rejoice because of the freedom that flows in me. Thank you for washing out self-destructive blame, guilt, and unfounded remorse. I will live hydrated by your living water and with my heart drenched with your unconditional love. In Jesus' name. Amen.

Reflection Questions

- What keeps you drained lately?

- What do you thirst for?

- When will you allow Jesus to set you free?

I Declare Out Loud

I affirm that I will not entertain any guilt because I missed days in this 30-day courage regimen. I refuse to let shame or any feelings of guilt enter my heart. Rather, I will declare that God is using what I learned, what I read and what I embraced to grant me the renewed life of boldness, courage and bravery I now possess.

Janet Perez Eckles

Part III
The Change Still Shines

Congratulations! You completed the 30-day plan. You persevered and you demonstrated tenacity and faith to reach the courageous, new you.

As this change came to your life in stages, the maintaining of the new you will also need support and inspiration and encouragement.

But you're not alone, nor do I want you to think that you're without support to continue the journey.

First, God's power at work will not stop. And His grace will not end.

Second, I plan to join Him. So, going forward, this new path you're in becomes part of your new life. And I'm here for you so the world's lures and temptations won't filter through and steal what you achieved in these 30 days.

I invite you to choose from the following options what you need, what you find feasible or what fits your life style.

- You can choose to have regular one-to-one contact with me during coaching sessions. This will keep you on track so the new you can see new potential, new horizons, and fresh opportunities.

Coaching details:
www.janetperezeckles.com/#!coaching/cy3r

- I will be honored to continue to minister to you weekly with my blog posts. You can sign up to receive my posts at: www.janetperezeckles.com/#!blog/c503

- Sign up to receive my videos that offer short and powerful inspiration to keep you going here: www.youtube.com/janetperezeckles

Let's Stay Connected

My Cyber home: www.janetperezeckles.com

Be my friend on Facebook: www.facebook.com/JanetEckles

[In Spanish] Quieres ser mi amiga? Facebook en Español: http://j.mp/1guSfIS

Follow me on Twitter: @janeteckles

Invite Me to Speak

Do you have an upcoming women's conference gathering, professional group event, or Sunday congregation?

If so, I'd be honored to deliver my message of empowerment, triumph and joy.

More details at:

www.janetperezeckles.com/#!janet-eckles-speaking/mainPage

Author's Note

What an honor to include you as part of my family of readers. The books I write and the insights I share are for you. I have you in mind when I pen each insight so they can be another stepping stone toward your life rich with contagious courage, with God's abundance, joy and success.

As an author, international speaker, life coach and radio host, my passion is to ignite in you a passion to always see the best of life. Let's keep in contact, I'm here for you: www.janetperezeckles.com

I welcome your comments and questions:
janet@inspirationforyou.com

P.S. If you enjoyed this book, would you consider leaving an honest review on Amazon?

Other Books I Wrote for You

Simply Salsa:
Dancing Without Fear at God's Fiesta.

Trials of Today, Treasures for Tomorrow:
Overcoming Adversities in Life

Hola, Happiness:
Finding Joy by Dancing to the Melody of God's Word

And Coming Soon

Fearless Faith:
a book to free you from fear, worry and anxiety

45015456R00052

Made in the USA
San Bernardino, CA
30 January 2017